EYES ON THE LORD

To Tony

DUNCAN BASIL

Eyes on the Lord

View of a contemplative

ST PAULS

Acknowledgements

Sea Fever used by permission of The Society of Authors as the literary representative of the Estate of John Masefield. Milton Shulman, *The Ravenous Eye* (Cassells, 1973), used by permission

Cover illustration:
Reproduction of wax painting by the author, Duncan Basil

ST PAULS
Middlegreen, Slough SL3 6BT, United Kingdom
Moyglare Road, Maynooth, Co. Kildare, Ireland

© ST PAULS (UK) 1994
ISBN 085439 476 1
Printed by Biddles, Guildford

ST PAULS is an activity of the priests and brothers of the Society of St Paul who proclaim the Gospel through the media of social communication

Contents

Introduction

For better or worse, Cistercian monks have long been known as "Contemplatives", as religious of a contemplative order. There are many who do not like the term since it seems to be of recent origin and does not, perhaps, adequately describe our monastic way of life. Some think it would be more correct to think of us as "listeners" since Mary at the feet of Christ was there listening to the Word of God Incarnate rather than just looking, contemplating him. And, after all, our Rule of St Benedict opens with the command "Listen" rather than "Look".

For all that, we are generally known as a "Contemplative Order" and it is from this point of view that this book is being written albeit in a rather Humpty Dumpty fashion. Humpty claimed that words meant what he meant them to mean and it must be confessed from the start that "contemplation" is at times stretched to unusual limits.

True to form, the book begins with a picture-story, something that can be looked at, contemplated and held in the minds-eye as themes develop around the central idea – the power of vision, of contemplation to transform life and its behaviour. There is no harm in a cat looking at a king but if it stares too long the consequences could be serious. Here, then, is an attempt at a concrete vision of spiritual realities in this elusive area of the contemplative life.

1

At the gates of Paradise

Tell me where is true love bred
Or in the heart or in the head?
And if it is by true love fed?

(Misquote-Shakespeare)

We stood there the two of us, worn out and tired by the long terrible ascent – stood there beneath the great spreading Cedar that grows by the Gates of Paradise. To our right the track fell steeply towards the Valley of Purgatory, hidden now behind a huge outbreak of crag and rock. To the north, thousands of feet below us we could see the flame and smoke of Hell, so remote that through this clear, crystal air of Paradise, it looked almost beautiful.

Wearied, silent – we listened.

"And what were you," came St Peter's voice, "down there on earth?"

And in strong Cockney accents came the answer, "A bus conductor, Govnor."

"And did you bus conduct?"

"Not 'arf I did."

"Then come in," said the Saint, "There's plenty of room on top."

Half apologetically, as if by way of explanation, he added to us, "You see, if a man is true to his vocation in my Church, if he does what he is, so to speak, then he becomes so like that great Shepherd of the flock that I just can't refuse him entry."

Even as he spoke a Dominican came up beside us, his black cloak a little singed by Purgatory, but yet a certain spring in his step.

"Ah," said St Peter, his eyes warming at the sight of a religious habit, "Domini canis, one of the Lord's own hounds – and did you bark down there?"

"Fifty years of preaching," was the mild reply.

"Did you study?"

"Four hours a day."

"But did you growl at the Jesuits?"

A pause – then the O.P. shuffled and looked down. "Yes", he said candidly, "I'm afraid I did – a bit."

"Fine, fine," came the answer, "keeps them up to the mark; come on, come on in."

It was only now that St Peter seemed to realize that we too were awaiting his scrutiny, and he turned towards us, his seaman's eyes appraising at a glance the cut of our Cistercian habits.

As he turned, I noticed that the tapping of the Recording Angel's adding machine had stopped and from the room above the gate a curious combination of noises had taken its place. There was the clatter of wooden treadles, the creak of a small windlass and the regular soft, swishing sound of wood sliding over cloth. Seeing my puzzled look, my companion nudged me.

"A loom," he said.

"A what?"

"A loom – you know, for weaving."

In a flash I understood. You could tot up the good and bad deeds of most vocations on an adding machine and strike the balance for Heaven or Hell; but here were we, monks, whose lives were utterly dedicated and that you couldn't get on to any machine. Only the pattern and complexity of a woven tapestry could record such a lifetime. Even now the angel was weaving the record of our lives; each cross-movement of the shuttle, one day nearer the end.

"Ah!" said St Peter, "contemplatives." Then, like a thunderbolt, "And did you contemplate?"

We were aghast. "Did we what?"

"Contemplate," he repeated stubbornly.

"Your Grace," muttered my companion desperately, "we were just ordinary Cistercians."

The Saint rounded on him fiercely. "There is no such thing as an ordinary Cistercian. Why, in all England my Church has barely three or four houses dedicated to this unique vocation, so different from all others. No one else could do your work, no other spirituality but your own could support it. Nothing less than contemplation could make possible the love and suffering that was your privileged lot. Did I relieve you of preaching, teaching, nursing and parish work just so that you might wander about in an ordinary sort of way – with all those souls to be hauled ashore by your unique life of prayer and sacrifice? After all," he went on, more mildly, "was it so difficult or high-faluting?"

"Have you never seen a farmer of a Sunday afternoon, contemplating his fields. What did he do but gaze steadily, drinking them in, appraising them as a whole. Not the time now for activity or detail. Had he started to tie things up or attend to the ditches you would no longer have said he was contemplating his fields. There would be silence, no kids around, and – notice this – from that long steady gaze would come a growing love and appreciation for his farm. Then, more important still, the farmer would come, in time, to reflect his native soil in his own make-up. Why, you could tell a Sussex farmer anywhere, he is like his county – and how he loves it.

"Your farmer gazed steadily and from this contemplation love developed and from that love was begotten likeness between farmer and farm; a likeness that brought union so close that separation would have broken his heart. And from that union came the fruition of God's plenty; harvests such as only Sussex soil can carry.

"You, too, were to gaze steadily – on Christ. Day long he was there before you in the brethren; you really only met one Person all through those rambling corridors. Only one Voice really fell on your ears, not the ref book, the chapter or classes. No, only chapters of the same Book – the Word speaking, never silent. The manual work was his cross and way of providing alms; the choir his song; the scriptures his life. You, in silence, had only to gaze and gazing, to grow in love.

"Then, like the Sussex farmer, to become transformed by that love into likeness and union with him. Then, ah then, as the Doctor whom I gave exclusively to your Order as guide – as St Bernard told all who studied him – the Holy Spirit seeing Christ's likeness in you and your compassion for others, the Holy Spirit would have brought you to the Father."

The Saint fell silent and seemed lost for a moment.

"Father," he murmured, "Abba, Father."

Through that stillness sounded the decisive snicker-snack of scissors cutting through cloth, as the Angel cut the tapestry off the loom. Peter looked up.

"What's it like," he called.

No answer. But the Angel – such is their privilege – came straight through the wall holding the tapestry in front of him by its two top corners.

There was our life. Running through the length of it, the three great strands of Faith, Hope and Charity; making complex pattern with these, the five vows; here and there bright splashes of colour, marking the sacraments. Ah – but what a mess. You could see that the tapestry should have been fine embroidery but want of recollection had coarsened it to sack-cloth. The great lines of the vows were irregular and tufted by infidelity, the deep pile of silence showing only here and there, mostly at the annual retreats. The whole was worn thin and shabby by constant talking. We hung our heads.

"Perhaps," said my companion, "its better on the other side."

Peter cast an enquiring glance at the Angel who looked down at the side we could not see, he paused for an instant as if something had caught his eye, then slightly shook his head.

Eternity – Heaven or Hell – and we stood there silent. Yet one word was still ringing in my head. "Bernard, Bernard," and I turned to the troubled Apostle.

"Do you think, Holy Father, we might see St Bernard, just for a moment?"

"Last I saw of him," said the Angel, "he was working out a new ending to the Salve with St Augustine and when those two get together there's no getting any sense out of either of them." However, at Peter's nod, he faded through the wall.

A few moments later came a quick, eager step; a great smile of welcome for our Cistercian habits – then a shadow of pain as Bernard's eye caught the tapestry. For a second his glance seemed held by something – but he straightened up, serious and pained.

"There's only one Person in heaven who can manage this," he said. "Wait here." And he was gone.

We waited, miserable, and to pass the time the great souled Apostle showed us a trick he had learned on the Sea of Galilee. How to tie a reef knot in a piece of string with only one hand. But you could see his heart was not in it and none of us felt like telling him it was a granny.

Then Bernard was back again. "She wants to know only one thing," he said. "Have you seen my Son?"

We stood there blankly. At least we did. Not so the Angel. Their wits are faster than ours and he was clearly tremendously excited.

"Look," he said and as we crowded round, his finger moved rapidly over the tapestry, tracing out, through all its shabby defects, a dim but unmistakable outline – till now unnoticed, so faint the impression.

There, by the grace of God, woven from the stuff and confusion of a human life-time, was the Image of her Son, the only pattern of Christian life on earth – Christ crucified. There as we gazed at the tapestry, we saw before us a copy of the Shroud of Turin, that mysterious enigma of today.

"Come," said St Bernard, motioning us on into the glad assembly of the saints, "Come let us tell Our Lady that we have seen her Son."

Tell me where is true love bred?
In the heart and in the head;
And it is by gazing fed.

2
Unpacking the story

A Chinese proverb maintains that one picture is worth a hundred books and, though it seems a pity to comment on the obvious, a few remarks may help to make things stick. St Peter, who has a heavy responsibility as doorkeeper, is concerned with the key to the Kingdom, with the criterion of Heaven. Did you respond to God's call by fulfilling your vocation in life? Did you do what you were – bus-conduct if that was it, preach if a Dominican friar? As for us, Cistercians, the mind-blowing probe, did we contemplate? Today, when a more social scope has crept into spirituality, he might be taking a different line. "Where are the others; those you met on the pilgrim way – for I was poor, hungry and sick and did you respond in love?" It is even possible that he will scrap the questionnaire approach and produce a stethoscope, anxious to know if we have a warm, beating heart in place of the pre-baptism heart of stone. But all this is conjecture since the story is pre-Vatican 2, and we have to take it on its own terms.

The recording angel is there to stress that time does matter and that life is "not a tale told by an idiot, full of sound and fury, signifying nothing". It does have a purpose. Each humdrum day is shot through with the call, with this vocation to be about the Father's business in a contemplative way. Every cross-stroke of the shuttle adds a day to the tapestry of our lives and its no good talking about "routine living" since each passing hour is necessary for the final pattern. But why a tapestry at all? And here, in the age of the laity, we must apologise for the story's exclusive presumption which saw the consecrated life as the sole province of the religious life and not as the goal of every Christian. Only a tapestry seemed capable of presenting the mysterious complexity of a religious life whereas you could tot up the merits and failings of other vocations on an adding machine and strike a spiritual balance – so many missed Sunday Masses in debt as against the merits of lifelong patience in raising a family.

St Peter got very hot under the collar at the monk's astonishment that judgement was about to be pronounced on such a hazy matter as the contemplative vocation. After all, what was it; all this talk of gazing and mooning around? You could not really judge on such a vague issue – they were just ordinary Cistercians, floating along and keeping the Rule. Despite his active fishing vocation, the angry apostle was insistent that Mary, the contemplative, had a real part to play in the Church's mission. Released from all active ministries such as preaching and parish work, they were to concentrate on the one thing necessary – love. And here he cottoned on to the theme of this book that love is rooted in vision, in attention and in contemplation. "Tell me where is true love bred... and it is by gazing fed." The picture of Dante smitten by the mere sight of Beatrice comes to mind and epitomises the truism of love at first sight. Vision and love seem intertwined and the consequences can be serious for, in some mysterious way, vision transforms life and we become what we love. They say that there is no harm in looking but love makes alike. Whatever beloved holds our habitual gaze is likely to mould us into its likeness for better or for worse.

To clarify the issue, St Peter took the example of a Sussex farmer of pre-mechanised days. Here was one who looked at and loved his land; here is one who gradually began to take on the gentle, generous contours of his farm and here is one who so loved it that its earth responded with rich Sussex harvests. Love is always fruitful and by his fruits you judge the measure of this farmer's love. A silent transforming process is at work here and not only of the individual but also of the whole locality. He enjoyed God's plenty but the county too was enriched by his loyalty and love. It was this love that inspired others to make Sussex the farming haven it once became.

And so for the contemplative. He should have his eyes fixed on Christ for, after all, time passing is Christ passing and by the gaze of faith one could see and love him all along the road of life. He was there in the brethren, there in the servers in the refectory, there in the sacraments. We encountered him everywhere and had only to gaze and grow in love, letting the transforming power of contemplation form in us this likeness.

St John put it succinctly, "We shall become like him for we shall see him as he is."

But the fat was in the fire for the tapestry was in the very devil of a mess. There were the shabbily kept vows, the poor silence, the mean measure of faith, hope and charity. Hope, of course springs eternal in the human heart and there was just the chance that it was better on the other side. No such luck and, confronted by the evidence, there was nothing to say. In tight corners, the average Cistercian will always have recourse to St Bernard but at the sight of the tapestry even this doctor of the Church felt helpless. Only his lifelong love, the Blessed Virgin, could possibly cope with such a crisis. And he was gone.

Mary, of course, is always concerned with the one thing necessary. She is looking for the family likeness, for the image of her Son and if that is there, Hell itself cannot prevail. Was the life of Christ crucified discernible in our lives? On the tapestry this had escaped St Peter, St Bernard and ourselves but the angel, with quick angelic wits, spotted at once the indistinct outline of the saviour's work in the tangled mess. Baptism and a wobbly fidelity to vocation had implanted and woven into our lives the likeness of Christ. There was the facsimile of the Shroud of Turin, there was the passport to Heaven because there was the image of her Son, Christ crucified. And the heavenly Father, like his Mother, is looking for just this – the family likeness of his Only Beloved Son.

The misquotation from Shakespeare is trying to express all this in a nutshell. In whatever mysterious realms true love is bred – in the heart or in the head – one thing is certain, it is by gazing, by vision, by contemplation fed. The vision of faith can lead to love and, in the process, transform us into likeness and union. From that union comes fruition – God's plenty for the soul and for the Church as a whole. One question remains. Are we, like Mary, like the Magi, like the Shepherds contemplating Christ with the eye of faith and so allowing the power of vision to transform us into his image and crucified likeness?

3
Professionals

Much of the difficulty in dealing with the contemplative vocation stems from the rather hazy notions conjured up by the name. It's easy enough for teaching or nursing religious to give some account of themselves but what of the contemplative, the gazer, the silent stay-at-home?

Some years ago we were brutally challenged on this by a famous psychiatrist who stared at us and demanded, "Who are you people? What makes you tick; what makes you get up in the morning? Why did you come here?" Our rather feeble answers were torn to shreds. "We provide some kind of Christian witness to the world." "My wife and I do the same." "We live by the gospel counsels of poverty, chastity and obedience." "So do my wife and I." "People come from miles around to see our lives." "The same happens at the zoo."

Had we been less taken aback by his frontal attack we might have turned on him for, fundamentally, he was in the same situation as ourselves. "Why did you choose to get married? Was it for money; witness, security or sex? Who and what are you? He had to be careful with his answers since his wife was there in the room with us. The truth was that we were both in the same boat and there was no functional or practical reason for our choice of vocation or for his. Contemplatives may witness to the world, they may be power houses of prayer but the only real reason for their calling is quite simply love. Presumably the psychiatrist, too, married for love and his wife would have been satisfied with no other answer. Just so, the monk, in his turn, can give no other reply however inadequate it may sound to a highly technical and functional society.

Put briefly, the psychiatrist and we ourselves, were each called to a special life's work in a school of love, he as a married man and we as contemplative religious. Both had made solemn profession of their chosen state by vows taken in public and, as a result, both might be called professionals in the art of life.

It is perhaps this image of the professional person that best unravels the mysterious business of a vocation and especially that of the contemplative. The professional is one who has heard a call and feels compelled to answer with a life's response. It may be to the sea, to land, to medicine or the law, to teaching or to the arts. You hear them saying that they just had to answer the call, to nurse or to farm, nothing else seemed to matter. The call can come to the surface as a kind of inborn charism – the sea was in his blood; she had green fingers or music in her finger tips – and we call such persons "naturals". Masefield has caught something of this in his poem "Sea Fever".

*"I must go down to the sea again, for the call of the
    running tide
Is a wild call and a clear call that may not
    be denied."*
*And all I ask is a windy day with the white
    clouds flying
And the flung spray and the blown spume, and the
    sea-gulls crying.*

It is a wild call, a clear call and a call, of course,
implies a response, a deliberate choice which is going
to amount to a dedication of life's energy to one spe-
cific goal. And this profession is going to stamp its
name ultimately on the one who answers. He becomes a sea-man, a farm-er or a law-yer as if the
element he chooses begins to enter into his very bones.
This is no private affair for it affects the whole community. It is a public profession of a life-style which
is why you do not go to a lawyer for pills – you look
for the doctor's brass plate. Such a dedication is costing and demands radical sacrifice. If you choose music
you die to the law and have to put in hours of daily
practice that exclude much else. If you choose the
sea, you give up home for years of life and, if marriage, you give up the club. In the preparation for
such vocations there is a kind of death to find professional life. The average undergraduate or apprentice
is in for hours of study and must cope with run-
down digs and shrill landladies. He must submit
willingly to much correction and probably go half
starved. Graduation or qualification, like solemn monastic profession, comes as a kind of resurrection from
studentship or novitiate death.

Now this mention of the professional brings us

back to the contemplative theme. The distinguishing mark of a professional is surely a kind of deep absorption with his profession. Despite the activity it may involve, his inner vision is held by the vision of his vocation. He is, in fact, a contemplative at heart. Most of us have seen a scholar deeply absorbed in his books; have watched an artist lost in his painting or have wondered at the night-long vigil of a caring nurse. It is something that came home to me in a curious fashion during an instructors course on flying training. The dry, objective and official manual notes the possible causes of lack of progress in a fledging pilot. "Is he sick? Is it just a matter of incompetence?" Then, out of the blue, "Is he in love?" All the world knows the intensity of lovers' contemplative gaze and the consequent impracticability it entails. They drop plates, forget the clock or pancake on landing. And in any professional circles, the talk swings back to the same vocational vision – they talk shop, endlessly. In the last resort a professional's reputation depends on this pre-occupation, this gaze upon, his life's work. He is at heart a confirmed contemplative and one would be very uncomfortable with a surgeon or pilot whose mind was not on his job.

The curious thing is that gradually a man's profession begins to work back upon himself. It begins to transform his outlook and become a basis of comparison for the whole of his life and it shapes even his vocabulary. Sailors do not die, they "kick the bucket" or in more jovial moments they "splice the mainbrace". We feel "out of sorts" quite unaware that it is a technical term in printing and first applied to health by professionals in that trade. A farmer once rang up our airfield to tell us that "one of our airyplanes had settled in his cabbage patch" as if it was just another kind of large cabbage white butterfly. It is clear from all this that some deep transformation is going on as life and professional choice are beginning to interact.

It does not end there. Vision begins to transform one's very personality and the stereotype begins to emerge. You do come across the precise and perhaps dry lawyer formed by precise laws and dusty documents. Most of us have known the wise family doctor whose long experience with human ills have mellowed his scientific training. There used to be the wise and slow old farmer type and there still persists the forceful ex-head mistress. The order, discipline and wisdom of any profession moulds personality and all know the quiet assurance of a professional person in times of crisis. Vision has done its transforming work.

It was Donne who gave us, "No man is an island" and no one's vocation grows in isolation. People are watching the watcher, gazing at the professional or contemplative and gradually the locality begins to be affected. Towns and countries become famed for a product – Dutch masters, Swiss watches or even the homely Yorkshire pudding and its all because one person was held by his vision and others were looking on.

Gradually this group of onlookers forms round a founder until the original hermit of a West Minster becomes famous and his locality, a City. Vision has not only transformed an individual but has formed a community.

All of which bears directly upon the vocation of the contemplative religious. The only difference being that his gaze is held, not by something, but by someone. He has made his profession not to a career,

25

to a trade or to a craft but to Jesus Christ. As St Paul puts it, "The love of Christ drives us on" and this is more than a kind of natural talent or acquired skill. It is a grace. It is, in fact, the gift of the Holy Spirit, poured into our hearts at baptism and differentiating itself as the call to a contemplative vocation. The call of the sea or of medicine can be powerful enough but this is the call of an Infinite Person, an infinite thirst crying "Come to the Father." Baptism makes the Christian a natural for God and the contemplative vocation calls him to become a professional in the art of vision, "It is your Face I seek, O Lord."

So the monk has heard "a wild call, a clear call that may not be denied." Against all logic and entice-ments, Christ holds his gaze and, like the Sussex farmer, offers him the whole transforming power of vision to unite, make alike and to make fruitful both himself and his locality.

The harsh truth is that there is no substitute for the professional's gaze of love. We try all kind of less demanding alternatives: fidelity to a law or rule, ac-tivity, strict observance or even psychology. But none of this will do. Wrong diagnosis by a doctor or crude stitching by a seamstress may offend us but what is really offensive is the lack of love and love's commit-ment. It shows up in poor attention and shoddy workmanship and we say "his heart is not in his work, he is not really interested." The one thing necessary is missing – that absorbed gaze of the lover and there is no alternative.

The strange thing is that poor technique and fin-gers-all-thumbs are no barrier to love. The Cure d'Ars had no teeth, no skill in preaching and much of what he said was distressingly trite but the love of God in him was so evident that France flocked to his church. Miracles and conversions were the order of the day. Love's inner gaze can make good the fumblings of natural clumsiness and the quality of the contemplative's life will depend primarily on the steadiness of his gaze. Mary treasuring all these things in her heart points the way and her assumption reveals the goal of the contemplative's vision.

4
Two contemplative laws

Cistercian monks are buried without coffins and as I go down on the single plank beneath my back, maybe I will sit up and shout, "I've got it." After years of pondering this mysterious business of contemplation, the answer to St Peter's question, "Did you contemplate?" will flash through my mind. As that moment has not yet arrived at the time of going to press, one can now only mull over its implications. Were we men of vision, characterised by that professional and absorbing gaze? Did we see the truth of things with the eye of faith, catching sight of God's invisible nature and so grow imperceptibly into the likeness of his Son? Or were we blind to God, to reality and so engrossed in our own little earthly kingdom as to be living in the classic Zen state of illusion?

St Benedict called it a state of "oblivion", of forgetfulness as we nod through life, eyes closed and half asleep. And his Latin "omnino semper effugiens" – always, utterly escape from it – is desperate with the insistence that we should wake up, run like mad and rub this terrible slumber from our eyes. Shut eyes cannot see God, cannot do the contemplative thing. They can only miss life's true mark. "Awake thou that sleepest and arise from the dead and Christ shall give you light," light to fulfil your vocation to see and be transformed.

There is a pressing need for answers because the contemplative has a great responsibility in the Church. If the contemplative is the "eye of the Mystical Body" and if his eye is "dark" then what of the darkness in the Body itself? His vocation is meant to spread out and illuminate the whole locality and if his gaze is dimmed then "where there is no vision, the people perish."

At first sight, there seems to be no difficulty about contemplation since sight seems to be automatic. You have only to open your eye and you cannot help seeing. Join the Cistercians, so to speak, and up you go. But when you come to think about it, sight is seldom an automatic reflex. There is an active element involved, a willed choice to focus attention on some particular object. If there is a ship out at sea, you have to squint into the sunlight to see it, oblivious to the sea-scape around. If there is a friend standing before you, you do not fix your gaze on the wall behind. When the "Exorcist" film was first shown, many in the audience covered their eyes, they did not want to look. Contemplation in any field of life demands a real choice and, for most of our lives, we see what we choose to see. You could formulate it as a kind of law that we see what we love, what we want, what we choose.

And the choice of life's gaze leads into an inevitable transformation of the "seer" himself. If you walk through the fields with a butcher, he does not see the frisking lambs, only lamb chops. Walk through the woods with a carpenter and he is blind to their beauty as he gazes on so many cubic feet of useful timber. When we got our first camera we no longer saw "Mum" in the viewfinder but a good snap – the chosen object of our then desire. The Zen people have put it well in a puzzling proverb, "a pickpocket, meeting a saint, sees only pockets". The thief is not interested in holiness or holy men, only in cash and his eye is on the pockets that hold it. He sees what he wants, what he chooses to see and the irony of it is that a St Francis is probably penniless.

Christ is telling us to walk with him but our gaze is distracted. As St Bernard puts it, we are "curvatus", bowed down with eyes glued to the earth. We think we walk alone, oblivious to the Christ at our side. We do not believe his assurance that the pure of heart shall see God and this beatitude, so special to the contemplative's heart, goes unheeded.

Sight, then, is not altogether automatic but selective and the first law of "spiritual optics", of seeing what we choose and love, inevitably leads into the second. We tend to become what we choose and love to see. Contemplation has this power of transforming personality and if we look too long at violence we shall probably become violent. A cat may look at a king but if it keeps staring, there's trouble brewing. Kings cannot stand rivals with swelling heads. They say that there is no harm in looking but if you page through any of the shiny county magazines you notice with sorrow that horsy women, in the end, begin to look like horses. And in real life they even begin to neigh at you.

A deep, radical and imperceptible transformation of personality, for better or for worse, is the inevitable consequence of the professional or contemplative stance. You see it at its best in the classic example of a Darby and Joan. A couple's married life has become so much a matter of mutual regard that each begins to take on and share in the characteristics of the other. Their handwriting begins to look alike as does the very way they walk. Ask one a question and the other answers in the mind of the other. One feels like a cup of tea and there it is to hand, unasked. Mutual regard has led to likeness and union so close that their fairy tale ending becomes almost credible. Two similar trees growing over the stream of life and uniting into one to grace the fields of Paradise.

Contrary to the usual notion, there is a dynamic element to the contemplative life. It is not Mary just mooning around at the feet of Christ. A deep sea-change is going on in an area of life that psychology recognises as the most difficult of all to modify – personality. St Paul puts it like this. "And we with unveiled faces, reflect like mirrors the brightness of the Lord always growing brighter and brighter as we are turned into the image we reflect. This is the work of the Lord who is Spirit." And as if to ram the point home, the Jerusalem Bible adds a footnote, "The contemplation of God in Christ gives the Christian a likeness to God." Selective seeing has worked its mysterious power of transforming personality.

Every profession involves its own discipline, which is as true for the natural contemplative as for the religious. There is a kind of transcendence about the two laws of spiritual optics which cannot be escaped. He must be constantly choosing what he wants to see and then be submitting to its transforming power. And that discipline will demand a certain kind of life-style which is very familiar to a long monastic tradition.

There will be a need to hold and steady the heart's gaze on its professional goal in a kind of loving awareness. This means that he will have to ignore much else by neglecting the distractions that swarm like flies about the mirror of the mind. "Recollection" was once a very familiar word to describe this concentration and was, in days gone by, rightly stressed. Then there will be a need for silence and for the inner quiet that allows the soul to reflect reality as in the still surface of a lake. As an Irishman once remarked of a piece of poor workmanship, "Sure, a blind man on a galloping horse would never notice it." He was really saying that a steady platform is needed if you are to observe with any degree of precision. That is why silence and stillness are so associated with the contemplative life and it is the deep meaning of the psalm verse, "Be still and see that I am God."

Ultimately the contemplative like the professional must be submitting to the transformation which begins to see life and even creation in terms of his chosen profession. Then he will begin to catch sight everywhere of God's invisible nature. The Church Fathers used to reckon that the universe was a kind of illuminated manuscript revealing on different levels the nature and designs of God. You could gaze on him always and everywhere. The spiritual eye would begin to see him in the woods, rivers and trees and this would be the equivalent of admiring the beauty of a manuscript without as yet understanding its meaning. Insight grows deeper with closeness to God, and the text of the book of creation becomes intelligible as one grows into the "mind of Christ". He begins to fathom the depths of God, to read the signs of the times and to walk constantly in his sight. Just so the contemplative is asked to discern Christ present in nature, in the scriptures, the Eucharist, in the brethren and even in the personal history of his own life. An inner gaze, so held, is graciously moulding him into the likeness of his life's choice and desire and he begins to see and speak of life in terms of his chosen profession.

On a more practical level this discipline calls for a constant scanning of conscience. When and where, today, did I last see his hand at work in my life? He is not a God of the gaps but an ever present Father, always concerned and always at hand but we tend to see him only in the more dramatic events of life. The saints, heaven help us, were often aware of him ever present at their side or in the depths of the soul. St Margaret Mary never sat down, unless others were present. She was always so conscious of his presence and holiness that you always found her on her knees or flat on her face. It can help us lesser mortals to preview the day and so be readied for those times, like the Eucharist, when he is most likely to be apparent. Hopkins puts it well, "For I greet him the days I meet him and bless when I understand." The two laws, in sum, are always calling us to redirect our gaze, to choose again to see what we love and to submit to a graced transformation into the likeness of Christ.

5
The world gone contemplative

Many years ago I was heading for Africa in search of a site for a new monastic foundation and I knew that I would be asked time and again for a description of the contemplative life. It would have to be in fairly simplistic terms for it had not yet been seen in the locality I was to visit. And that set me thinking.

It was then fashionable to liken a monastery to a royal palace where court liturgy was the order of the day. The regular choir offices were an expression of that formal obeisance due to royalty, while the manifold liturgical rites and regulations were the etiquette proper to Christ the King. There was some truth in such a presentation in that it did not try to see contemplative life in functional terms. It demanded knight's service rather than hope of earthly gain. But in this democratic age kingship has a bad press and makes little appeal.

There was a time when the monastery was popularly known as a kind of power-house, generating spiritual electric current for the various activities of the Church – light for the teachers, sound for the preachers, warmth and light for all. It was a very impersonal expression of a very personal way of life and the description got us into trouble after the African monastery had been founded. The interpreter who was translating my efforts to sell this idea got it wrong and for years after we were invaded by nice young men looking for a job in the bicycle factory.

Some liked to stress the power of a contemplative monastery to witness but the idea of being goodies on a pedestal for the world's admiration hardly appeals to the average monk. Again, St Thomas Aquinas put things very clearly. He held that the religious life was the creature's greatest response to God. It was the free and total gift of self to the Creator which is the basic reason why we were created. It is a rather chilly, theological formulation that Africans probably would not have appreciated.

In all these descriptions, the contemplatives element is rather played down as being a late and non-patristic terminology. For some, the word "contemplation" has overtones of a vague lifestyle which, for the ever-practical African, poses the question, "How contemplate an invisible God?" Really, it would have been much easier to meet Africa's curiosity had we been medical missionaries with their practical nursing skills. Or, had we been Dominicans or Christian Brothers we would have been accepted eagerly for the educational needs of that young continent but here we were, contemplatives. There seemed no real analogy, no striking illustration to identify us in the world's eyes.

Then it suddenly struck me that, for the first time in the history of the human race, an unprecedented example of our contemplative vocation had emerged. The world itself had gone contemplative and television aerials on every chimney top witnessed to the fact. With the coming of the box, millions of people had their eyes glued to their chosen vision and are getting lost in a secular version of the contemplative life. The parallels and consequences are uncannily alike as they demonstrate the transforming union that vision begets.

Every time TV is switched on, Law 1 comes into play for a choice has been made to see what one loves, often for hours on end. Slowly and imperceptibly Law 2 then does its transforming work and, like the Sussex farmer, personality begins to change and take on the characteristics of the beloved vision. For better or for worse, the mind-set of an habitual TV viewer has grown light years away from the far off, pre-television days and this came home to me years ago when talking to Bill, our farm manager.

"Bill," I said, "How do you get on with TV?" "Well," he slowly replied, "At 2.30 after Saturday lunch, my wife and I sit down before the box to watch the sport; she pushes in the tea-tray at 4 pm. Supper comes in on a trolley and sometimes we stay there till midnight. Of course, if there is an international soccer match, we will sit up till 2 am to see the end of it." And I thought, "Here on our monastic doorstep is a real, non-stop contemplative." Like Mary Magdalen at the feet of Christ, he was at rest, doing nothing and absorbed in his vision from afar. By the simple act of switching on he had made a selective choice of what he wanted to see and, all hiddenly, the transforming power of vision was at work in his life.

Perhaps the effect of such sustained gazing at TV

was more evident in the early days as we watched the emergence of the "television teenager" a new type of youth. It was then long hair, jeans, dagger shoes and an inbuilt restlessness that drove our local photographer to distraction. "You can't take quality time exposures today. My young clients just can't sit still." Often a kind of superficial boredom seemed to have dampened their natural enthusiasm and, when visiting our pottery, they would pass by the miracle of a pot growing out of the potters hands with – "Oh, we've seen it all on telly." Milton Shulman puts it well. "It must be evident that any child brought up in the TV age, any child who spends 22,000 hours between the ages of 3 and 18 watching the small screen – who spends more hours under the influence of the box than of its parents, its teachers or its priest... any such child must be different from a child who was born and reared in a non-television age." Here is vision transforming personality and often in a horrific way. "In 1964 the Ladies' Home Journal estimated that the average American child has witnessed on TV the violent destruction of 13,000 human beings, mostly during the children's hours between 4 and 9 pm." If the basis of DIY is "Show me how its done", then so many horrific demonstrations may well explain the prevalence of violence today.

The world, then, has followed the monastic tradition and gone contemplative. It is gazing on its beloved and growing alike with the inevitable consequence that the locality, besides the individual watcher, is becoming transformed. In this country alone probably millions will be watching a top rating programme. This means that all are looking at, thinking about, talking about and perhaps acting out in fantasy one and the same vision. Viewers are becoming so like-minded that recently an historian claimed that TV did more for the unification of Italy than any previous revolution. It levelled accents, broke down county barriers and gave Italians a single political and common vision.

Contemplation is doing more than producing like-minded individuals for it is quietly bringing community to birth. Among perfect strangers who have never seen or heard of one another, this silent attention is forming a kind of mystical and electronic body of the BBC. A multitude is becoming of one mind and heart and if you have banned TV from your home, you are out of it. Parents trying to take such a line find that the family is living in another world, not talking the same language or thinking the same thoughts as their neighbours. They feel, as one father put it, "excommunicated". "Today," Shulman goes on, "suddenly, because all the peoples of the world are parts of one electronic TV network, young people everywhere share a kind of experience that none of their elders ever have had or will have..." Inevitably, community forms because shared experience is the very basis of local or global community.

There is one final and cheering step in this likeness between religious and secular contemplation and it might be reckoned as Law 3. It is simply that contemplation is a mutual, a two way, affair. Lovers have eyes for each other and the gaze of any contemplative is precious in the eyes of the beloved. Once again, the analogy with TV holds with almost creepy precision. The BBC is anxiously and intently looking at its viewers. Hence all those popularity polls and the mysterious electronic counters that reveal how many are watching a particular programme. The Corporation is desperate to know who is looking at and contemplating it. If you were to ring them up and tell them that your kids were delighted with last night's show, they would coo with delight – "It's very kind of you to say so; it's good to be appreciated; we always try to do our best. What intelligent children you have." They would be hugely pleased at such attention because contemplation is mutual, desirable and reciprocal.

The contemplative, then, is not just looking at God in Christ. God is looking anxiously at us and craving our attention as any father or lover would. He knows that the highest compliment of adoration or love is to be the centre of another's attention. You see it in Mary, defended at Christ's feet, and you see its lack reproached in the garden, "Could you not watch with me for one hour?"

The media age, then, is clearly telling us a lot about how to go about our life since it too has gone contemplative. First comes selection. Law 1 requires us to choose what we love and want to see, Channel 1 of the BBC or for us, God in Christ. And then, in stillness and perhaps much darkness, Law 2 begins its transforming work as we assent to the vision. If it is a soap opera, then there must be the submission of belief that is required if any story is to be accepted and enjoyed. And this finds its counterpart in the spiritual life in the assent and submission of faith. It is a kind of docility which permits the transforming effect of vision on the contemplative to take place. Finally there dawns the cheering realization that contemplation is mutual. We are not just gazing into an unresponsive void and this is the assurance of Law 3. The BBC, in its own small way, is delighted to be the object of our loving contemplation just as God is craving for the attention of his children. "It is my delight to be with the children of men, playing in the world." As we look towards him he is looking anxiously at us so that the whole contemplative process can be at work, transforming us into his likeness in a union of love that is always, by his grace, fruitful.

For the first time in history, modern technology is presenting us with a tangible symbol of the contemplative life and the power it has to transform the world. TV viewer and religious contemplative might well both take as their theme song, "Drink to me only with thine eyes and I will pledge with mine." All said and done, the children of the Light can indeed learn from the shrewdness of the children of the World.

6
Practical contemplation

So far we have discussed the transforming and unitive power of the contemplative vision upon the individual, the locality and the community. A miser's heart grows as cold as his gold – he becomes what he loves. Silent and gazing millions, unknown to each other, become of one mind and heart in an electronic family of viewers. This family is fondly regarded by the TV company because contemplation is mutual and draws watcher and watched into an embrace of mutual love and admiration. Such is the unitive power of contemplation and "Drink to me only with your eyes" might well be the plea of God the Tremendous Lover.

The difficulty, of course, arises when we try to put all this into practice. The run of the usual monastic day seems to offer little opportunity for such a quiet lifestyle. Time is short, bells are ringing and the brethren's needs demanding. You begin to wonder if it is possible to square Mary's quiet repose with Martha's crowded day? Can you really be a contemplative in the average mayhem of a monastery?

Once again ordinary human behaviour can give us clues and we can learn a lot from the familiar hi-powered businessman – the "jet-executive". Despite the fact that he is busy with phone calls, pressing interviews and flight bookings – despite all this, he is actually totally recollected. His inner gaze is held and focused upon a single goal, the "main chance". This is usually the next step up. He is going to get on and get up and nothing is going to stop him. A university graduate in ICI once remarked that, in the office, they were all so polite and so well bred until promotion was in the air and then it was nature red in tooth and claw. Nothing can divert the executive's vision. There may be deadlines to meet and pressures to resolve but the main chance is always before his eyes. The vision is revealed as the director's swivel chair or, as Anna remarked in "Mister God", that's the shape it makes as a hole in the human heart.

How, on earth is the monk to take all this on board? Well, St Paul solves the problem, "my just man lives by faith." This eye of faith gives us the power to penetrate the surface of things and see the spiritual reality beneath. Faith is like an X-ray camera which reveals the bones of God's will under the flesh of daily events. So often the monastic day seems to go haywire. You sit down for a quiet half hour of spiritual reading and ten tons of fertilizer arrive, to be off-loaded at once. You put your feet up after a hard morning's work as guest father and a party of fifteen school children is announced. They have had no dinner and one of them has just been sick. All the multiplying villainies of nature seem loaded against contemplation but nothing can baffle the X-ray eye of faith. It can see God's plan beneath all this in a silent and steady gaze upon his will. Nothing but rebellion can dull this contemplation in faith and it comes as a great relief to know that activity is no bar to one's basic vocation. Its not so much a matter of being still but of loving attention.

It may sound grim, but love is really a union of wills to which loving attention gives witness. You do not have to be totally recollected before loving a friend. It's much more a question of "What do you want; what would you like to do this afternoon?" and it is the leit motif of Christ's life. "I always do the will of him who sent me." No activity, busyness or sickness need disturb this union and synchronism of wills which the eye of faith X-rays beneath the surface of events. This came home to me one day as I passed by an airfield where the Red Arrows were displaying their incredible formation skills. I suppose they were flying along at some 200 miles per hour through all their complicated aerobatics but, despite this speedy activity, the planes were dead still in relation to each other. Their flying was so synchronised that you got the impression that they were locked together by some kind of invisible link and all the while there was this curious contrast of stillness and activity. It all depended, of course, on a union of eye and will as each pilot fixed his gaze on the leader, intent to do precisely what he wanted, no matter how complex the manoeuvre. It was a powerful demonstration of the contemplative gaze uninterrupted by speed and activity and it was an assurance that Mary's quiet could live with Martha's busyness. Love is basically a union of wills and the contemplative, despite a hundred and one demands, can always "formate" on the will of the leader.

If the X-ray eye of faith is switched on through all the twists and turns of the day then the whole run of contemplative gazing begins to operate, even in midst of mayhem and hassle. We are choosing to see or at least glimpse what we love; we are therefore being slowly transformed by grace into his likeness and he is delighted because this mutual exchange of attention is all that lovers crave.

It is at this point that a nasty little niggle intrudes. Can you formate on an invisible leader? Attempts to formate in dense cloud usually end up in near-disaster with planes spilling out of the cloud all higgledy-piggledy. Can we unite our wills with the "God we cannot see"? As the hours pass by you begin to wonder if I have seen, heard, or experienced his will today? This is urgent because love depends on this union of wills and where is my leader now? With the pagans we begin to wonder, "Where is your God?" and sometimes must confess, "heaven knows!"

Despite all this, the Spirit is ever trying to develop in us a sense of God's Fatherly presence and providence. He is trying to make manifest that cry, hidden in our hearts, "Abba, Father". The birds of the air are kept fit and well and the lilies relieved of spinning yet we doubt his caring will for us. We are like the average insurance company which will cover you for just about everything except "acts of God". These turn out to be quite extraordinary events like tidal waves, earthquakes and now, alas, radiation. Anything less than such spiritual upheavals in our lives are dismissed as chance or coincidence and the Father's unceasing care goes unseen unless the roof falls in. Only then do we grudgingly ascribe our escape to a vague, impersonal providence. All the minutiae of daily living

like, food, clothes and friends can be X-rayed by faith
and seen for what they are, a Father's loving care. Our
usual reaction is, alas, "I've had a Hell of a day." This
is theologically and chillingly exact since Hell is the
total absence of God. Day long we have not recog-
nised him or his will and contemplative transformation
into his likeness has slowed to a standstill.

Yet the Father persists. Christ is always with us and
the Spirit ever pleading in our hearts so that there is
nothing chance or accidental in anyone's day. Every
moment is part of the vision, an aspect of God's will
calling for our formation if only faith will open its
eyes. Life is not like the grandfather clock repaired by
one of the brothers and ticking away but, as he remarked in wonder, "It's going alright but I still have
this wheel and I don't know where it fits!" There are
no spare parts in creation only hidden mysteries waiting for the discerning eye of faith and the transforming
power of vision.

It is possible then to be practical about this rather
elusive contemplative vocation even though the
busyness of most monastic days seems to militate
against it. Faith can always be holding the Main
Chance in view and recognising the will of the Beloved disguised in the trivia of the day. Its not perhaps
the steady gaze of Mary at Christ's feet but such
glimpses are a measure of practical contemplation
which permit the transforming and fruitful power of
vision to take its course. The Sussex farmer was not
always Sunday-idle and the Mother of God, contemplative though she was, nonetheless hurried to the
hill country to assist Elizabeth like any other busy
and practical "Mum". There is a time to be still and
see the Lord but, during the intervals, the gaze of

faith X-rays the day to catch, beneath the surface of events, glimpses of the Beloved.

Perhaps the most inspiring incentive to this kind of practical faith is to be found in chapter 11 of the Epistle to the Hebrews with its mysterious opening verse, "to have faith... is to be certain of the things we cannot see." It was by a kind of second sight that Noah, under the Middle East's scorching sunlight, foresaw the rains and built his ark – a very practical demonstration of faith. In such faith Abraham left house and home and Moses the splendour of Pharaoh's court whilst others put up with mockery, chains and prison. They were X-raying the events of a cruel and workaday world, "catching sight of his invisible nature" and keeping the Main Chance always before their eyes. And the contemplation of their vision led to some powerful transformations of personality such as Jeremiah, a Christ-like figure, prophetic of the Suffering Servant to come. As for the individual, so for the transformation of a rabble of slaves, leaving the bondage of Egypt and becoming at last the community of the People of God.

Sometimes, and only sometimes, there is almost no need for an X-ray camera as the events of life seem to coincide with a clear vision of the will and ways of God. Here is an instance and I imagine most people can recall in their lives, something of the sort.

It was time to return again to Africa and, for a change, I thought I would fly out dressed in the Cistercian religious habit rather than a clerical suit. Rather secretively, I wondered if the reception I got on the journey would be any indication of what the Lord was thinking about it all.

At Birmingham airport a security officer, with some

kind of electronic wand, was searching me for weapons when he stopped short and said, "Father, are you from Caldey Abbey?" "No," I said, "But I have been there and am in fact a member of the same religious Order." "Well," he replied, "I know Caldey well; come on, Father, you go straight through." This seemed a good start to my faith journey. At Paris, I changed to Air France and some-where over the Sahara desert, about lunch time, I was just paying for a can of beer when the head steward came hurrying down the centre aisle of the plane. "Father," he said, "Its so good to see a priest in his soutane, I am paying for your drink." Not long afterwards he returned and, without knowing anything of my flying career, bent down and asked if I would like to meet the captain. I remarked that in these days of hi-jacking and dressed in this medieval costume I might look like some kind of terrorist. But he would take no refusal and led me onto that holy of holies, the flight deck. The captain happened to be a French Canadian so we were able to have a long technical talk, in English, on the handling and navigation of modern jet aircraft.

After about twenty minutes of this I pointed out that he would soon be coming into Douala and would be pretty busy. So we said goodbye. "Lord," I thought, "You really are showing your hand."

As I left the flight deck, there was the head steward waiting for me and with him one of the stewardesses. "Father," he said, "What's it going to be; a whisky and soda or an iced champagne?" I opted for the iced champagne as the most appropriate way of celebrating such a manifestation of the Lord's approval and we spent the rest of the flight discussing the merits of plain chant, for both of them were Catholics. On landing, I said, "Lord, I think you have made your point."

There was little need to X-ray the day in all this but for most of life we walk by faith and have to formate on the glimpses we get of God's will in the humdrum events of life. But glimpses can coalesce into a habit of discerning Christ passing by and this very practical form of contemplation then works its transforming alchemy as we grow in his likeness and into his community.

7
The desert

By now we have droned on at length about the necessity of prayer and about the transforming power of the contemplative gaze. There has even been some kind of hint that the spiritual life is basically a love affair. Nonetheless, if we are honest, we have to admit that there has seldom been so much as a sniff of the supernatural and that consolations have, on the whole, grown rarer and rarer. As one novice master used to remark, "You cant depend on FIF; it fades." By which he meant a funny inside feeling. More galling still is the fact that the harder we try, the worse it seems to get as a growing sense of the absence of God silently replaces his presence. God seems to peter out. Like professionals, we may have tried to conjure him up by studying books or like lovers turned to the "love letters" of the scriptures but he is nowhere to be seen, heard or felt. There has been a steady advance into a desert of total absence and once again the psalmist seems to mock us, "Where is your God now that the vision has faded and there is nothing to look at, nothing to contemplate?"

It is a crisis time. Our reaction is to go rushing off along a non-existent path towards a desert mirage. We might strain to squeeze out a drop of devotion or to give up scripture for the more emotive field of novels. There is a constant temptation to disillusion as routine begins to displace the living bond of personal relationships with God. It is a time when monks jump over the wall, nuns go hysterical and parish priests threaten the bishop with nervous breakdowns. In short, we get into a state.

The irony of all this is that we have forgotten God's immemorial way of making friends and forging covenants. Just think of Abraham. "Leave your home, leave kith and kin, leave familiar and absorbing occupations and come into exile. The toys and dolls of this world have become your idols. The Promised Land awaits you even though the road home runs through the desert." In the desert Joseph the Patriarch was sold into slavery and in its sandy wastes a whole people spent forty years before emerging as the People of God. He did not spare his own Son those forty days of desert temptation and this was followed by a lifetime of exile on this earth, far from his heavenly homeland. So with us, God is at it again. "Leave home, independence and all the things you trust in; come into the desert and there turn to me, the Living God and to nothing else."

The book of Hosea tells us that it was not chance but God's cunning to lead his wife into the desert, into a spiritual vacuum of aridity and mess. There, in anguish and despair, she would eventually turn back to her Beloved. The desert is the place where God can fashion his friends if only they will trust and stay put. The whole tragedy of Saul was that he would not trust, would not wait for Samuel but gave up hope and lost his kingship. God is persisting still. He is determined that we should love him. He takes immense pains to get us into the desert of absence, darkness and desolation for the desert is the great proving ground of love. Quite simply, it poses the question, "You love me when I am present but what if I am absent?" A wife might wait years in the hope of her husband's return from a war, spending the time in keeping house and home together and in marital fidelity. On his return, her constancy in love would be plain to see for nothing so proves love as fidelity in absence.

If God feels exasperated, he might well be excused. Here we are calling this most valuable, this most carefully planned and essential desert the "end of my spiritual life" when in his Fatherly providence things are just beginning! Our natural reaction is that the desert is a funny kind of place in which to make love – most lovers would prefer a cinema. And the same questionings arise when we open an old copy of the works of St John of the Cross. There, on the first page you find etchings of fat little friars, dangling their sandalled feet over the edge of a sheer precipice. Smiling complacently, they are waving you on along a road into arid desert wastes. Written on the road are the words, "Nada, nada," which translated into plain English means, "Sweet damn all." Just what is God up to and "where are the leeks and the onions of the cosy little spiritual life we once knew so well?"

It might solve some of our difficulties if we took a hard look at the desert since there is obviously some fascination, some lure and even truth about it. Down the centuries men have been torn between love and hatred of the desert. Often you detect in the Old Testament a note of nostalgia for those idyllic desert days when Israel was so close to Yahweh. Lawrence of Arabia could never get the desert out of his system and my own experience of it resonated with the strange paradox of attraction and revulsion evoked by its aridity.

We were a desert squadron of twenty-four aircraft, squatting in some godforsaken area south of Tobruk. Flimsy tents were no protection against the sweat and heat of the day or the zero temperature of the night. Enough water daily to clean teeth, shave and wash – in that order – and little else to eat other than dehydrated spuds. Sand everywhere, in your hair, books and machinery. Your nightmare climaxed in the certainty that the scorpions and asps could climb the legs of your camp bed. Just once a week there was the faint hope of a bottle of warm, imitation beer.

Each eleven-man air crew daydreamed of the rare two weeks leave in Cairo, the glittering city which offered all that the desert lacked. You would meet them on the eve of departure, full of glee, pockets bulging with cash – no shops in the desert – and all fixed up to hitch-hike on a plane flying back to base for maintenance. Cairo! There you really could get a bath; there was the cinema, green grass, the cool majesty of the Nile and there, above all was Groppi's. This dream restaurant specialised in nothing but ice cream from the lowly cone to a three course meal. Hot chocolate sauce, poured over the lot, was an exotic and optional extra! At Groppi's, you had come home to the city.

Oddly enough and just one week later, you would find the same crew wandering around the desert camp in a sheepish kind of way. "What's up? Thought you were away for a couple of weeks. Has the Nile dried up?" "Oh, we got bored stiff and so fed up we hitched back again." The plain truth was that, even on the natural level, the pleasure, comfort and lure of the city were insufficient and contemptible. There was something in these young air crews that wanted real issues, dedication of life to a single common purpose and the city had failed them. It is a hunger that cannot be stuffed with ices and rather bashfully they would ask if there was any operational flying that night.

That perhaps, is the first great lesson of the desert – we do not live by bread alone and it is as true for the spiritual desert as for the dusty wastes of North Africa. The excitement, pleasures and activities of the world cannot fill the vacuum that God makes in the heart. In some such desert alone is there the liberty and realization of the need to come to grips with the true purpose of life. Inevitably Augustine comes to mind. "Thou hast made us for Thyself, O Lord, and our hearts are restless until they rest in Thee." There is a deep, obscure revolt of soul if we try to cram it with the ice creams of our own sweet will. The hunger of the human heart is greater than the city can fill.

And the moral of all that? In desert times, think twice before jumping over the wall, before threatening the Abbot with a nervous breakdown or simply opting out. God's predilection for deserts as the trysting place of love has not changed.

It is, of course, possible to make the journey in the reverse direction, to go from the city to its sandy wastes. As you left the luxury centre of Cairo and headed for Alexandria, there was a lightning deterioration into shanty-town as the road passed the pyramids with the sphinx smiling dispassionately into the sky. You met the homely Arabs, ragged and tied up with bits of string. Their camels were roped head to tail, snobbish and disdaining despite this evident insult to well-bred pride.

You are on a lorry and heading for the desert to man a radio beacon designed to guide aircraft home from long operational flights. The black, tarmac Alex road stretches out ahead, flanked by featureless, sandy wastes. At milestone 70 you go into four wheel drive, turn off the road, set the compass due west and keep the speedometer at a steady 30 miles per hour. After a couple of hours, by this dead reckoning navigation you should be at Point X though there is nothing to say so, nothing but oceans of sand. The lorry off-loads your rations, camp bed, water cans and radio unit. It then roars off in a cloud of dust.

Your first job is to dig a hole slightly smaller than a grave and not quite so deep. This gives you head room under the canvas if you sit on the edge of it, feet dangling in the hole. You pitch the tent and think of going for a walk – but give up since there is nowhere to go. As you sit there, uncomfortable thoughts begin to emerge. If that lorry sets the wrong compass course, if it gets shot up by enemy action, if it does not return – then I die. I may have splendid physique, I may have an exceptional IQ and many skills but left to myself – I die. And the second, stern lesson of the desert comes into focus – a rude sense of my own insufficiency. I am forced to admit that by myself I cannot cope and if left alone, I die. Our theology tells us that we depend on God, that created out of nothing we would fall back into it without his support and that we are saved by the redeeming work of Christ. All of which is true but tends to remain a pious notion until some kind of desert experience has branded it on our souls. It is a fundamental blow to our pride and self-sufficiency.

The desert comes in many disguises such as misunderstandings, rejections or sickness but love's purpose is hidden in all this. Ultimately the desert is telling us, in the only language that really gets home, that we need a Saviour and without him, we can do nothing.

Until Peter started sinking, he probably thought he was a pretty competent fisherman and not a bad chap. Paul had great ambitions until struck off his horse and the Magdalen was tops until some terrible remorse hit her at his feet in Simon the Leper's house. It seems doubtful if repentance is possible until the desert has totally convinced sinners that left to ourselves, we die. And in that realization, the peace of Christ is born.

8
The desert blooms

A week or so of sitting at a spiritual Point X is sufficient to persuade one of the hollowness of the contemplative life. Vision has vanished like a mirage and nothing remains to be seen across the sandy horizon. St Peter's question, "Did you contemplate?" has become an irrelevant mockery and the contemplative gaze into empty space suggests the onset of madness. And yet there is wisdom, there is purpose in these desert and desolate places.

A small speck of dust appears on the horizon. It grows and rises high in the air. It comes closer and ahead of the small sandstorm you begin to make out the ugly outline of a desert truck. A kind of wild exhilaration surges up within you and, as it swirls to a dusty standstill, you pat the bonnet of the old bus with a burst of real affection. A friend in a need so desperate is a friend indeed. And that is the first positive lesson of the desert, the first sign of its Spring blossoming. It has forced you to look outwards and brought you from the despair of self-sufficiency into that first stirring of love which is gratitude. Despair was gnawing at your vitals and hope "had grown grey hairs" but a saviour has come to the rescue and the vision reappears.

It really was love's trick to lead Hosea's wife into the desert where she would turn to me in despair, look outwards and respond in gratitude. We too, gritty from long sitting at Point X, have so often found spiritual bread, perhaps a little stale, or water enough, though muddy. A hidden mystical presence has been feeding, clothing and sustaining us and out of such life-experiences is born a hope that mere theory cannot conceive. A Father, a Saviour, a Power has come to the rescue and now we can witness to the good news with conviction. What pearls lie scattered in our spiritual wastes.

In fact, some kind of desert seems to be the contemplative's natural habitat like fish in water and yet we are always misinterpreting it as the end of my spiritual life or the death of self-fulfilment. But it is so clearly signed with the sign of the Cross, so clean with the hope of resurrection as to be the perfect place for single-minded gazing on Christ. And if we are looking at him, he is there looking at us with delight. This assurance of Law 3 of mutual contemplation is confirmed by Our Lady. Joyfully, she reminds us that he looks on his servant in her desert nothingness.

There remains one more positive lesson before leaving these sandy wastes of a dead end spirituality. It is another reason why the air crews used to return early from their city leave. The desert is the abode of the Spirit, a place of companionship and community. Nowhere, in all the comfort and ease of Cairo would you find the same cheerful, grubby and unwashed bunch of ruffians as in a desert unit. The spirit of a desert squadron was almost palpable. Aircraft were worn out, tools scarce and no spare parts yet the response was terrific. In the blazing sun, where you could literally fry an egg on a plane's wing, you would see ground crews, stripped to waist, cheerfully sweating away to get aircraft serviceable for evening operations. All they needed was tea galore as they worked and whistled, doing the impossible.

Even on the natural plane there is a spirit which only the desert seems to generate. In such sparse conditions each one's life depends on each others' generosity and such constant mutual sacrifice flowers into a comradeship of deep appreciation. It brings to mind the descriptions of the Early Church where "they were all of one mind and heart" and it grows into an invisible bond of astonishing strength.

This came home forcibly to me one day when I had to take a plane back to the maintenance depot in the Delta area. Taxying to a halt, I slid back the cockpit window and asked the warrant officer if he could get the machine serviced by next day. We were short of aircraft and the need was urgent. He looked at me with utter astonishment and spluttered out that it was Saturday afternoon and the men were going to the cinema. Thinking of those ruffians in the desert, I sagged and felt totally flat at this sudden descent into bourgeois city life.

This then is the strange power of the desert, the power to form and give birth to community. It had fashioned a military unit just as it fashioned ragged tribes into the People of God. It had engendered a sense of one's personal inadequacy to go it alone and out of this had grown compassion, self-sacrifice and comradeship. Maybe only desert experiences can teach us real love and fellowship in place of the tendency to go through the motions in a series of spiritual exercises. For the desert is the abode of the spirit which, in the spiritual desert, is revealed as the Spirit of Love.

That does not promise us a deck chair and the simple life but challenge. The desert fathers went out to single combat with the evil spirits for the desert also belongs to them – hence its barren desolation where nothing good grows. St Anthony went even further and lived for a while in an old tomb since that was the place of the devil's triumph, the place of death. Here he could really challenge Satan and, in the power of the resurrection, struggle and overcome. Christ the Galilean carpenter agonised there for forty days against Satan and emerged victorious as the wonder-working teacher. He was so filled with the Spirit of love that he finally fashioned the wood of the Cross to our salvation. In our small deserts there is often a twist to our temptations that betrays, not so much our own infidelities, as the presence of these evil spirits. And the agony, the struggle is not simply against our personal sins but against principalities and powers. It can be a desperate struggle, an agonia, for the spirit of this world is clean contrary to the spirit of God. But out of such grace-won combat comes strength and confidence – just one more blossom in these desert wastes. St Paul sums it up, "Trouble produces endurance. Endurance brings God's approval. His approval creates hope. This hope does not disappoint us, for God has poured out his love into our hearts by means of the Holy Spirit, who is God's gift to us."

The desert then is not the end of my spiritual life but almost its very condition for it is the shadow of the Cross. It makes us wise, grateful, loveable and beloved. It enticed crews back early from leave sickened by the lures of the City, having discovered their hunger for real issues. Point X smashed the idol of self-sufficiency, taught us to look outward for that lorry. Gratitude was born from its saving presence as it is born from the growing experience of the Saviour's hand in our lives. And in the desert, as in the humdrum world, others agonise and they need us as we need them, life given for life. Out of such service and compassion blossoms life's most precious gift, the spirit of friendship and community. The pattern did not change even for Christ for it was out of the desolation of "Eloi, Eloi," that the Spirit was given to us under the mysterious life-giving signs of breath, blood and water. In that desert at the foot of the cross, community was born – the Church, the new People of God. Our task, like that of his Mother standing there, is to trust, to wait and to pray through long, dusty hours because "There in the desert, I will speak to your heart."

9
Busy and quiet prayer

St Bernard seemed to think you could reconcile Martha's busy day with Mary's restful hospitality on the grounds that they were sisters. They should be able to live together. But even among sisters tensions arise and most of us have felt them in the average monastic day. To some extent faith can resolve these stresses as it discerns the will of the Father in activity or stillness. Faith can always formate on the Leader in a union of wills no matter how complex the manoeuvres, knowing that there are no spare parts, nothing trivial, in the designs of God. He spoke, in the beginning, and creation tumbled into being so that things, like words, are meaningful. Quite literally there are "sermons in stones and books in the running brooks." The contemplative in busy times can always gaze on events and circumstances and say, "Yes" to the Word hidden and revealed in them. Events invite a response and the question is really "Will you won't you, will you won't you, won't you join the dance" whether it washing-up or feeling washed out.

Behind this approach is the classic book by De Caussade, "Abandonment to God's Providence". He held that every moment of life was a kind of "Sacrament of the Present Moment". Just as the minute hand of a clock is telling the present time so each moment of the day is pointing to and telling us the will of God at this very moment. He calls it a "sacrament" because the sacraments are outward signs, like water or oil, of inward graces. A splash in the baptismal font indicates that another child has joined, in a hidden way, the Kingdom of God. The present moment is therefore a kind of sacramental gift, carefully wrapped up in the brown paper of very ordinary circumstances. Faith alone can unwrap the parcel and discern the gift within. Faith sees and greets the God always present which means that the contemplative gaze need never be interrupted and its transforming power can continue throughout the busiest day.

De Caussade calls it the sacrament of the "present" moment because it is only this moment of time that really lies in our power. No one knows what the future may bring and few can control it. The past is over and gone as Lady Macbeth realised after the murder, "What's done cannot be undone..." There remains only the present moment to which we can say yes or no and to lovers, the great contemplatives, this moment alone counts. It's not "Did you love me yesterday," or "I might love you tomorrow," but "Do you love me now?" So we have the "Sacrament of the Present Moment" in which faith's X-ray gaze discerns, greets and obeys its chosen Vision, the Main Chance. "Time passing is Christ passing" which means that the gaze can become habitual and Martha, troubled by many things, can be at peace with Mary, resting at

Christ's feet. Both, in their ways, are attentive to the same Vision.

The snag is that de Caussade also calls it the "Sacrifice of the Present Moment" because he knows that Love's call comes to a selfish world and to selfish hearts. The Father is asking us to give and we are determined to grab so that there is always a confrontation in doing his will. "Let Thy will and not Mine be done" as Christ, in his agony, three times expressed it. "Yes" to the present moment is a choice that involves continual sacrifice as we bend our wills to the manifestation of his as the minutes tick by. It "begins to burn the clothes off your skin, the skin off your flesh and the flesh off your bones" for God is a jealous God and wants "me" and not my worldly goods. It is really no wonder that a small girl once asked, "Why, Mummy, is the will of God always so horrible."

We have to make a choice of "Yes" to a vision that is often repugnant or grumble our "No" which is the sad way down to dusty death. It is some encouragement to remember that lovers and saints delight to do the same thing, for better or for worse. A lover will willingly bear exile with the beloved and St Paul glories in the cross of Christ because it is the pattern of his life and the trusting place of his presence. And it is interesting that he speaks of all this in the present tense of the Present Moment – "With Christ I hang upon the Cross." Here, on earth, the joyful sacrament of the present moment is accompanied by the joyfully accepted sacrifice of the present moment for we are looking to a Crucified Beloved.

There is, then a contemplative solution for busy, active Martha, for the bursars, the teachers and superiors of the average monastery. In fact most of us fluctuate between busy and quiet times and there seems to be a need to move from one kind of prayer to another to meet these changing moods. Busy times need a busy kind of prayer like the Rosary or those short, vocal ejaculations beloved by the desert fathers. But at quieter times, like the early morning or late evening, a much more restful prayer becomes possible. It's the still, silent gaze of Mary at Christ's feet which, though wordless, is yet working its powerful contemplative transformation and union. Perhaps the real art of prayer is to learn to move easily from busy to silent prayer as the day unfolds.

Most of us, though, feel the need for a simpler approach to the complexity of life, for a stronger anchor than the practice of the present moment. We want to move from activity to stillness and presence, to move from doing things for God to just being with him and this is a very authentic desire. If a friend is in the room with us, we do not think about or read about him. We do not pull out his photo and study it. His presence is enough and often silence or an occasional word is all that such personal contact requires. There is a felt need to sit around in church or a vague longing to be looking and listening in the kind of silent communion that lovers and professionals know so well. It is the prayer and silent communion of Mary of Bethany.

It might be called the prayer of presence – just being with the Beloved. For most westerners it is the most costing of all prayers and generates a wasp's nest of misgivings. "Is it just being lazy; nothing seems to be happening; I am making a muck of it so why not get up and do something useful?" The devil, of course, is delighted because the very aim and goal of prayer is union with God and he shrieks with laughter every time we get up and go. Against all comers, our first defence is simply to sit tight and be with the Lord.

All kinds of good things grow out of this way of praying, some nice and, curiously enough, some of them seemingly nasty. Its first effect is often a kind of tranquillity as all the soul's fragmentary desires are brought into unity by the simplicity of the contemplative gaze. And this seems to bring with it a "ghost-guessed" understanding of the meaning behind creation as God made and sees it. With this there comes, to some extent, an insight into the ways of the world, which, even in its worst aspects, begin to make sense. What we are not prepared for amid such tranquillity, is the creative shock that occurs when holiness comes close to those sitting at its feet. An advert used to claim that "Persil washes whiter," and it bolstered this up with a picture of two shirts, one grey and the other dazzlingly white. When the inaccessible light of God begins to shine on the soul its grubbiness becomes painfully evident. And this almost forces on us the precious but bitter fruit of repentance. You really do begin to realise what is nasty in the woodshed but once acknowledged, the way then lies open to closer union. Having said, "Sorry" a relationship can again blossom. You can then look the other in the eye and so allow the contemplative transformation to resume.

If such claims for quieter prayer seem a bit exaggerated then listen to some of the masters. Chapman likens it to the preoccupied gaze of lovers, so caught up in the one thing important to them, that they begin to drop things, potter about in a way that seems useless to the world about them. They seem to be doing nothing but if onlookers only knew...! Chesterton, who used to be found wandering around in the midst of London traffic, oblivious of its hazards, claimed that absence of mind was due to the presence of everything else. His interior vision was worth more to him than life and limb. John of the Cross reckoned that we, at quiet prayer, were like owls so dazzled by the sunlight as to think that it is dark and time to move off. All agree that God is close though we think he is absent as we fidget in the desert and darkness. But the will is united with his, formation is going on and this is not the time for busy meditation but for silence in the presence of God.

But our western minds, itching still for activity, go on asking, "What then shall we do?" And the *Cloud of Unknowing* answers, "Be intent upon God and none of his works," put a cloud of forgetting behind you and enter into the *Cloud of Unknowing* ahead for it is not now the hour to be thinking even about the mysteries of God. Why? Because he is very close and there is no need for much thought about your friend, there before you.

The truth is we are learning to pray more with our eyes more than with our lips as we gaze into the darkness of Christ's eyes, a darkness as profound as the depths of the Wisdom which he is. It is helpful to have a short word or phrase just to keep the imagination from clacking away because in times of deep involvement like this, we do not need to go into long explanations. If the house is on fire, the Cloud tells that you simply put your head out of the window and shout "Fire!" A short, single word says all and has a strange power of drawing us back from the lush fields of our daydreams.

It's a bit like driving along on a dark, wet night. You are straining your eyes to pick out the curb ahead through the beam of the headlights but the windscreen blurs up with the rain. Only when the wiper blade sweeps across can you peer clearly into the darkness. The wiper is our short word and when the screen of our imagination gets blurred and fogged by distractions, this word sweeps the mind clean for this dark contemplation. We are asked to let love's short word and love's steady gaze pierce through the night to the Presence before us.

It might be thought that such quiet prayer is really doing nothing and is no more than a lazy option but, like night driving, it can be hard and very demanding work. It can also be very boring to be with a silent or sick friend but presence suffices; it is what love most craves. Moreover this kind of prayer is going to take time. You need about twenty minutes for the mind and body to quieten before getting lost in it and there is a hint of the cost in Christ's sad words, "Could you not watch with me for an hour?" It really does seem to need an hour for its intimacy to mature. But beware, for then it can grab you for yet another!

The sacrament of the present moment has led us to the sacrifice of the present moment and beyond the busy prayer of Martha to the quiet and silent prayer of Mary. She has guessed that simply being with the Lord in silence is his greatest delight and her's, too.

10

Strangers, friends, lovers

It is high time for an assurance that there really is a theme running through all the meanderings of this book. Vatican 2's advice to return to our origins suggests that we look back for a moment to our starting point. St Peter was concerned to know if we had lived out our vocation on earth, had we done what we were – as contemplatives. Had we contemplated? Against all our protestations, he held that it was no more difficult than the task of any professional person and gave us the example of the Sussex farmer whose lived vocation illustrated the Three Laws of Spiritual Optics. As he gazed at his fields, loving what he saw, his vision began to transform his personality until eventually he begins to become alike to his farm and county. And in a sense the county is looking at him as its other farmers see and copy his example. Contemplation is mutual, as lovers know so well.

Then for the first time in history we found an analogy for the contemplative life. World-wide people are choosing, gazing at and becoming alike to the vision presented by the box. A community is forming of like-minded viewers while the mutual contemplation of Law 3 shows us the BBC anxiously looking back at its viewers, hungry for appreciation.

Our next task was practical. How to gaze steadily in the rat-race of a galloping world and St Paul answered by assuring us that the just man lives by faith. Faith can X-ray the day and keep the Main Chance of Christ steadily in view despite the baffling complexity of surface events. "Time passing is Christ passing" and the present moment is always revealing him in a hidden way so that the contemplative gaze and transformation need never come to a halt. If the jet executive, despite desperate activity, holds the director's swivel chair always in view – what of us?

St John tells us that God is love which means that, like human lovers, he wants nothing but love in return. It is the insistence of the Song of Songs that "my beloved is mine and I am his..." The trouble is that sin has estranged us. Though God still walks in the cool of the Garden we, like our first parents, hide away from his dazzling holiness. "I heard your voice in the garden and was afraid." We by sin have become strangers.

Our return to him becomes possible through his incredible grace but it is a progressive encounter, moving from estrangement to friendship until friends become lovers. It is the route we take in re-building any strained relationship; our prayer life can be seen as the means by which distance mercifully gives way to presence.

Take, for instance, the case of a stranger. Your brother has been called away suddenly and rings up to ask if you could look after his business partner for the evening. OK, but you realise that it is going to be hard work. You have never met this perfect stranger and have to start planning right away. A meal must be fixed up and you begin to wonder what you might have in common. What topics of conversation might be helpful to while away the evening. What is his background; has he any hobbies or is it going to be business only? As with the early stages of prayer, you have a lot of meditation ahead if you are going to make conversation with God and it can be very hard work. If your brother's partner is shy, silent or perhaps not all that bright then you are going to have to sweat. A simple "yes" in reply to your carefully contrived leading questions can lead to near despair.

We, by sin and infidelity, have to some extent become strangers to God and our prayer time and encounters with him are going to follow roughly the same path as dining a stranger. There's a need to tune into the mind of God through scriptural reading and there may be the need to hold some points in mind for meditation if our prayer is going to get off to a good start. There is a twist to the old monastic saying that to labour is to pray for this "stranger type" prayer can be very tough going. There will also be the slight awkwardness and formality that characterises any first acquaintanceship because at this stage we are getting to know about someone. We have not yet really got to know him for the person he is. "Do you know So-and-So?" "Well I've met him once at a party but I don't really know him?" It is going to take time and effort to move into the royal realm of friendship.

All these are essential stages in forming a friendship with a stranger but gradually things loosen up and we begin to know him rather than know about him. Conversation gets less formal and we forget to use the butter knife. Topics seem to bubble up from nowhere without a thought for previous meditation. Those dreaded silences are no longer desperate potholes but wells of intimacy and communion. A fundamental change is taking place as the other ceases to be a thing to wine and dine in the possible hope of business profit to your brother. He is emerging as someone unique and curiously loveable, someone you could begin to trust – a possible friend. Through dialogue, presence and that kind of communion which is akin to prayer, we are growing like-minded and united as we move from estrangement to friendship.

Its the kind of thing that most of us have experienced on a long train journey. You choose a window seat, gloriously free from other passengers until a "thing" plonks down opposite you. For a while you can keep it at bay with the larger kind of newspaper but then, hang it, you drop your spectacle case. The "thing" picks it up and the ice is broken; it actually begins to talk. At first the conversation is a bit formal; polite three cornered stuff about the weather, because both are cagey about getting involved. As the miles fly by, you gradually begin to discover the other person. "Oh, you are interested in bee-keeping; so am I. Did you see that article on swarm control; absolute nonsense. Good Lord, we are coming into the station. Here's my phone number; we seem to have so much in common. We just must meet up again." That two syllable word "we" signifies the silent transformation from stranger to friend.

This is the time when the French move from "Vous"

to "Tu" and when Englishmen start calling you "old boy," and it can happen rapidly. A police-car once followed me to the ruins of a nearby monastery which I was going to show a visitor. It parked behind me and a cap-and-booted cop stalked over to us and asked stiffly what we might be doing on this private ground. I explained I was from a local monastery and a total transformation took place. The cop took off his peaked cap, put his head through the window and whispered hoarsely, "What do you put on your onions? 'Orse manure?" I gave an inspired "yes" and roles flicked from a threatening and official stranger to a new-found friend.

As prayer-life deepens, we move from meditation about God to something more simple and personal because we are becoming aware of Presence. We are growing into an eye to eye encounter of "Thou" and "I" together and in this relationship silence replaces words. Gazing in contemplation is enough. Friends are finding one another and becoming "We" in the manner of lovers.

I once asked one of our African monks what the word to "love" was in the Ibo language and he replied, "Efonanya". I said that it looked like a compound word and wondered about its root meaning. "Well," he said, "I have never thought about it till now but 'Efo' is associated with light and looking and 'Anya' with someone, a person. I suppose our word to love really means gazing into the other person's eyes." And that was, I thought, the perfect definition of contemplation. It brought love and looking into a single context. "When you come to prayer," said the great St Teresa of Avila, "Look for the Other Person."

At this point we run into one of the categorical imperatives of life. If strangers to God or human beings are to become friends and lovers then they just have to find prime time to be together. Only presence satisfies lovers and maybe spiritual renewal and the deepening of prayer life depends on this costing fact. It takes courage and faith to drop some pressing activity and "waste" time, perhaps an hour, with the Lord "doing nothing". "My father," said David Kossof with enormous satisfaction, "had time for people."

Objections from our busy and competitive minds explode around us like an angry minefield. "You can't always be mooning about, wallowing in consolations – there's too much to be done." It is true that this kind of prayer can be a real rest as it brings peace and unity to scatterbrained body and soul but for the most part it is hard work. It can be an effort to begin, boring to continue and a relief to end. In short, it costs as does all giving and this is giving time to others. In the end, it is a cost that true love never counts.

As a small boy, on the way to spending the afternoon rigging up a radio set, I used to marvel at my big sister sitting on the sofa with her boy friend doing absolutely nothing. Worse to come. Hours later they would still be there wasting all that time so precious to my own little business. Decades on in life, I came to realise that wasting time with the beloved was really all that mattered. It was enough to be there, present, attentive and silent.

In times of crisis and temptation the thought of sitting still seems madness when frantic activity beckons as the only hopeful solution. Christ may have found some rival to himself in our hearts or the need for a drink is more urgent than the plain duty ahead. If we will only believe it, this kind of silent, attention can be the most effective shield against the slings and arrows of the enemy. "Lord, this really attracts me but my eyes are fixed on you," and walls of temptation silently melt away.

One of the most bedevilling difficulties, particularly to us golden oldies, is the tendency to nod off within minutes of settling down to pray. Sleep should be resisted but it can be a blessing in disguise provided we do not rush off on waking up. That brief forty winks seem to have the power to quieten the mind and allow Mary's contemplative gaze to be held peaceably by Christ. In these moments of dozing off, two further reassurances come to our aid. First, that children are probably especially loved when they are fast asleep, for one reason or another! Secondly, that by the Third Law of Spiritual Optics, contemplation is mutual and Christ is looking at his sleeping children with evident delight. In any case we stand to lose nothing because, in the presence of the Blessed Sacrament, the power is always going out from him to our great gain.

One curious fact that summarises this chapter is this. The run or progress of a longish prayer time seems to emulate that of the progress from strangers to friends and lovers. At the start of prayer the mind is busy and active, estranged a little by the dust of the day's distractions. As the minutes pass, prayer becomes quieter and a certain peace begins to herald the intimacy of growing friendship. And, sometimes, just sometimes, this merges into the prayer of the eyes, that wordless communion of Christ's Mother, "lost in contemplation".

Wherever we may be along the way from stranger, friend to lover, and despite all the objections, listen to that great Doctor of the Church, St Teresa of Avila. "Never, never, ever give up praying."

11

Thanks and praise

St Augustine noticed and once remarked that lovers tend to sing, "Cantare amantis est". He might have added that they tend to sing one another's praises and have no scruples in using divine attributes to do so. All Sylvia's swains "adored" her and it's common enough to hear that she simply "worships" the ground he walks on. Antony, talking of Cleopatra, pushed liberty with sacred language to its limits, "Age cannot wither nor custom stale her infinite variety". Lovers sing each other's praises and if the contemplative life is about loving then it must be characterised by this rather useless seeming business of praise and thanks.

Curiously enough such appreciation does not comes easily to the British stiff upper lip to whom the most glorious girl friend is simply "not bad". Nor does it feature much in the prayer of the average Roman Catholic, appalled by the enthusiasm of the "Are you saved" evangelical and worried by all that eternal harp playing on damp clouds. This reluctance to thank and praise is curious because it rises spontaneously in so many areas of life. Crowds pay big money to go to a soccer match, thankful for being able to get a ticket after all, and then they cheer their heads off at each home goal. Our first impulse on receiving a gift is to thank and then praise. Thanks without the appreciation that praise is expressing would be churlish indeed. "He said 'thank you' all right but not a word about the sweater I had made specially for him."

The theological roots of gratitude and praise go very deep indeed. If we are created out of nothing then we ourselves and everything about us is sheer gift. Appreciation would also seem to be the basic craft of human life. St Thomas Aquinas observed that every craftsman delights in the exercise of his craft and we think of our obsessive gardening friends or the quiet satisfaction of a cabinet maker at his work. Even in the animal world, dogs love to bark and ducks to quack as they do their thing and you would think that we humans would have a compulsion to be exercising our basic craft of thanking and praising the Lord for the fundamental gift of ourselves.

Our general reluctance may indeed spring from modesty or that fear of emotionalism crystallised, long ago, in the words of a bishop, "Enthusiasm is a horrid thing, a very horrid thing". But there may be deeper reasons for our caginess, some primordial instinct sensing that praise is a dangerous game. If you go into an African market and come across a heaped pile of the potatoes you are looking for, you go very cautiously. In England you might enthuse to the attendant that these were the very thing but in Africa you kick the pile contemptuously and offer half the price. There is a squawk of indignation from the mountainous mammy beside it and much haggling but eventually you walk off with your purchase at 75% of the written price. Had you said one word of praise or given a glance of admiration the price would have doubled. The moral of all this tells us that praise is a kind of deep assent. When you praise, you are saying "yes"; you are committing yourself, you are becoming involved and finally hooked and the mammy trader knows all about that.

Instinctively we fear to praise especially when it means "yes" to the committal of ourselves to a vocation like marriage or religious life because in so doing we must forego much else. We tend to side up with the Elder Brother who preferred grumbling to praise and in that "no" became isolated in his misery. It is not surprising if we neglect this dangerous game of praising when it comes to committing ourselves to a Crucified Lover; we can only marvel at St Paul's "glorying in the cross of Christ".

As if to encourage us, we find Scripture is full of gratitude simply because it is full of committed people who have said "yes" to God. Praise tells us that a person really means it, is deeply assenting and when Mary sings her "Magnificat" she is only elaborating on her "Fiat", her "Yes". How quickly the situation would have changed if only the Elder Brother had started to thank God for the return of his brother. How quickly our own situation would improve if continuous thanks and praise expressed the "yes" of our lives. But "yes" is a jump in the dark of faith and we fear its consequences.

It is cheering to realise that praise, for all that it is costing, can also be profitable. If you marry a millionaire then the world is your oyster because his money, his influence and power are now yours.

Lovers' praises are saying a mutual "yes" to each other and so to all the "worldly goods" involved. Christ's life was one of thanks and praise and even "on the night he was betrayed" he gave praise and thanks. In all this he was saying "yes" to the Father as the Father was saying "yes" to this Beloved Son so that it comes as no surprise to learn that "All I have is yours and all you have is mine." Sincere praise is so profitable that he could say "All power in heaven and earth has been given to me..." and it is out of such wealth that he invites us to "ask the Father for anything in my name", even for that infinite gift of the Holy Spirit.

It is curious that, at just those moments when we feel least like it, thanks and praise are often the quickest way out of the difficulty. Fears, doubts, depression or wounds begin to lighten, even if our praise seems a hollow mockery, for the simple reason that the "yes" of praise is the "permission" God seeks before he can pour out his saving power into the situation. The short, evangelical classic, "Prison to Praise" exploits this aspect of praise to the limit. Since God is a Father, everything is a gift; this tragedy, this trial, this spilling of tomato soup on your hostess's gown at a society dinner party – all is his gift, awaiting only thanks and praise before rushing in with his saving grace. It is the logical conclusion to St Paul's assurance that everything, even spilt tomato soup, works together for the good of those who love God and are fitting into his plans.

Perhaps one of the most cheering spin-offs is the joy that always seems to accompany appreciation. Praise may be costing or profitable but always carries with it a hidden smile. It really does take quite an effort to imagine thanks and praise being offered in a sepulchral voice from a deadpan face. In quite desperate times it does have this power, like music, to lift the spirit and revitalise its energies for the spiritual battle. It is poles apart from a kind of sad pharisaic approach to problems. This once came home to me in front of a huge pile of coal. It was waiting to be shovelled into the bunker on a dull, wet November day. My helper looked at it grimly and remarked in a flat voice, "Well, Brother, we'll just have to offer it up; there is nothing else we can do." God loves a cheerful giver and he would have been much happier with a praise approach than with this rather dismal holocaust. The ultimate paradox comes only with great sanctity. It is the real joy which the saints seem to have when suffering. It climaxes in their ability to praise God even when feeling miserable. In the midst of the next spiritual mess, try gratitude.

Finally, there is one very mysterious element about praise. You find it embedded in that psalm verse, "On the lips of babes, Thou hast perfected praise." And very oddly it continues, "to foil your enemies and foes". You wonder why praise of all things, even the babbling praise of infants, should have this power to baffle Satan and all wicked spirits that wander the world for the ruin of souls. There is a kind of victorious quality about praise and it is evident enough when a salesman knocks on the door. If your eyes widen and you start to sing the praises of his vacuum cleaner, he silently rejoices. Intuitively he knows that praise means "yes" and that the deal is done. To thank and praise God is to say "yes" to him and therefore "no" to the devil; and in that small "yes" victory is won. It has foiled our enemy and foes.

It really is sound advice to praise God in every

situation and come into joy for, if you choose the alternative and grumble, you are saying "no" to happiness. Devils cannot stand praise; when all in a room start to praise and sing they run like mad before such buoyant spirituality.

"In everything give thanks for this is the will of God concerning you," was Paul's advice to the Philippians and the contemplative can see this will at every turn of the day. Each response of appreciation releases a power and a pascal joy into our lives which hovers on the brink of song. No wonder that St Augustine noticed that lovers sing each others' praises.

12
Meetings

As the vision of the Transfiguration faded, we are told with a certain pathos, the apostles "saw only Jesus". In one sense, this is the basic occupation of the contemplative who is concerned all day long to see by faith "only Jesus". Some hint of the intimacy offered is given in the Ibo word for love, that "efonanya" which means to gaze into the other's eyes. But there is no exclusiveness in this relationship for Jesus commanded the apostles at the Last Supper to "love one another". He insisted that to see him is to recognise him also in others, almost to the point of identification. "I was hungry, thirsty, naked and you did not meet ME on the way." He is asking for that all-embracing love which is the inevitable consequence of contemplation.

Put rather flatly, you might say that life, and especially the inherent closeness of contemplative life, is largely a matter of meetings. It may be the casual bumping into people or the more traumatic business of stopping them bumping into each other but in either case meetings usually determine the mood of the dawning day. "The boss wants to see you." or "Don't go into the kitchen just yet." Life is mostly a matter of meetings and often they are its greatest trial or consolation. "Life would be perfect if only Br N were not here," and then by some merciful transformation late in life, you have to admit, "Thank God that Br N is here." The French say "Partir, c'est mourir un peu" because they know that to say "Goodbye" is to die a little and we all know that sense of diminishment and deadness when friends leave us and our meeting is at an end. Life is largely a matter of meetings.

Recognition and meeting are literally so vital that you sense the deep pain in a person's voice, as they tell you that they met someone in the street this morning and "he wouldn't look at me – he cut me dead." Rejection is deadly, a kind of murder, but recognition and welcome are life-giving and there is a feeling of well-being and vitality as we see a friend coming to meet us, hand outstretched. I once remarked to an old monk that gratitude would be the most fitting response to someone coming into the room bringing with them this aura of life; "Thank God for So-and-So." "Not thanks," he replied, "But Sanctus, sanctus, sanctus...!" It was if there was a hint of divinity about our workaday meetings.

In practice, all our encounters in cloister, work or guest-house seem to reveal a kind of Trinitarian element as if Christ the Second Person is trying to show us something of his home-life in Heaven. It is that personal touch which shows up in giving time, attention and eye-contact as we listen to the other. Quite unconsciously, we are imaging the Trinitarian dynamic where Person looks towards, and is given totally to, another Person in the Spirit of Love. In our human friendships this explains why "My friend is another myself." If you have given everything, including yourself – as happens in the Trinity – then identity and union with the other is complete. From this there often emerges that mysterious exchange of hearts that crops up in poetry, good or bad, spiritual or secular.

My true love hath my heart and I have his,
By just exchange one to the other given;
He holds mine dear and his I cannot miss
There never was a better bargain driven.

Meetings seem to mirror the Trinity and you see this at work when One Person of the Trinity becomes one of us, when the Image shares our image at the Incarnation. The Word Eternal is the same Person as Christ the Word made flesh and his whole human life reflects his eternal life with the Father. It is a meeting so intense that the Greeks give it a unique name – the circuminsession which St John describes in more homely fashion as "the Son in the bosom of the Father". It would be the same on earth. Christ's contemplation of the Father would never falter and at times he would deepen it by stealing away to be with him in prayer. His "food" was always to do the will of his Father, to do only the things that please him and ultimately he makes that final gesture of friendship which is total gift. On the cross, he gives himself into the Father's hands in the self-gift of death. His life was a poem of meetings with his Father. That was not the end for meetings are mutual and the Father responds with the gift of the life-giving Spirit at the resurrection. There is, then, this curious Trinitarian dynamic about Christ's life where an eternal contemplation and union are reflected in his human life and activity on earth.

It was the same when he came to meet, not only the Father, but ourselves. The Incarnation was a meeting of total intimacy with our human flesh and blood, so incredible that the Fathers used to say it was the cause of the fall of the Angels – they could not bring themselves to worship Almighty God lying in a manger. And at the Last Judgement, he has a perfectly clean sheet for he met us when hungry, thirsty and naked and cared for us "to the uttermost". We are being asked to see and love him, and his image in others, as totally as we love ourselves.

Since we are "made in his image and likeness" we find a longing for meeting that is universal in space and time. Aristotle reckoned that our earthly happiness lay not only in knowing the truth but also in having the companionship of friends. Jesus echoed him when telling us that eternal life and happiness lay in "knowing you, the One true God and Jesus whom you have sent." Real living, he is insisting, is a matter of many persons meeting and living as one. And, even on the natural plane, we long for company and are told that solitary confinement is a close second to capital punishment. And at just such a moment, on the cross, Jesus assured the thief that "this day you will be with me in Paradise" – they were going to meet again and for ever.

The nostalgia for unity is proof even against politics. Nations, from dictatorships to democracies, must claim it as their own. We are supposed to be the "united" Kingdom just as the States or the newly emerging republics of Africa feel impelled to incorporate "united" into their names. Lower down in the human scale come our Sheffield United, our Trade Unions and everywhere human beings rush into the perilous union of marriage. In short, there is a universal thirst for unity, the result of meetings, and a recognition of the fact that it alone makes life worth living. Christ's final prayer was a plea for this unity, "That they may all be one as you Father and I are one..." and the prayer was answered at Pentecost when the disciples became of "one heart and soul".

At the Last Day we shall not be asked "How was your spiritual life?" but how did you meet me on the way in the sick, the poor and the prisoners? St John takes a very ruthless line, arguing that to disrupt unity is to disrupt life. The man who hates his brother is not just a poor type but a murderer who has destroyed life itself. To the extent that we really meet people, life, natural or supernatural, increases or diminishes. It begins to dawn on us that our routine meetings are not some grim religious duty of offering each other up or occasions of gaining merit – they are sacramentals of that most fundamental meeting of the Three Persons of the Blessed Trinity. And we, small images of that great mystery, are programmed and commanded to do the same.

It may seem that so much insistence on meeting has taken us far from the contemplative theme but a contemplative community, if it is to remain true to its vocation, must be loving. It must be seeing and meeting Christ with the eye of faith for "true love is by gazing fed". It must choose to see what it loves; be transformed into the likeness of the Beloved and his brethren; and finally come to know that such contemplation is mutual and a joy to the Beloved.

Love like this is always fruitful because it is pouring out love into the Mystical Body of Christ in an unseen and unnoticed way. To be close to the source of a river is to be near its winding course and if you dye the spring, you dye the whole river. A contemplative community is like the heart of the Mystical Body. It can send life through the torn body of Christ even though it does not see or set out to do this. We may be power houses or the King's royal palace but love loves and the rest happens. You cannot harness love. All the world loves a lover but the lovers are too absorbed to notice the joy they are spreading. Like children at play, love cannot explain itself and the contemplative can hardly tell others what he is trying to do. He must get on with the work of loving God and others and to do that well, he must really meet them. It calls for prayer, attentive gaze and much silence. Then, no business of his, love will overflow and become fruitful. Torrents of Living Water can flow out from a heart or community that is transformed, by gazing, into his likeness; flow out to refresh a dry and weary world.

"Did you contemplate? Then come on, come on in for there is plenty of room on top."

Epilogue
St Peter's soliloquy

"Have you never seen a farmer of a Sunday afternoon, contemplating his fields? What did he do but gaze steadily, drinking them in, appraising them as a whole. Not the time now for activity or detail. Had he started to tie things up or attend to the ditches, you would no longer have said he was contemplating his fields. There would be silence, no kids around and – notice this – from that long, steady gaze would come a growing love and appreciation for his farm. Then, more important still, the farmer would come, in time, to reflect his native soil in his own make-up. Why, you could tell a Sussex farmer anywhere; he is like his county – and how he loves it.

Your farmer gazed steadily and, from this contemplation, love developed and from that love was begotten likeness between farmer and farm so close that separation would have broken his heart. And from that union came the fruition of God's plenty, harvests such as only Sussex soil can carry.

You, too, were to gaze steadily – on Christ. Day long he was there before you in the brethren; you really met only one person all through those rambling corridors. Only one voice really fell on your ears; not the ref book, the chapter or classes; no, only chapters of the same Book – the Word speaking, never silent. The manual work was his cross and way of providing alms; the choir his song; the scriptures his life. You, in silence, had only to gaze and gazing, to grow in love; then, like the Sussex farmer, to become transformed by that love into likeness and union with him. Then, ah then, as St Bernard told all who studied him – the Holy Spirit, seeing Christ's likeness in you and your compassion for others, the Holy Spirit would have brought you to the Father."

The saint fell silent and seemed lost for a moment. "Father," he murmured, "Abba, Father."